The Fun Book for Couples

OTHER BOOKS BY MELINA GEROSA BELLOWS

The Fun Book: 102 Ways for Girls to Have Some

The Fun Book for Couples

102 Ways to Celebrate Love

MELINA GEROSA BELLOWS

**Andrews McMeel
Publishing**

Kansas City

The Fun Book for Couples

Copyright © 2003 by Melina Gerosa Bellows. All rights reserved. Printed in China. No part of this book may be used or reproduced in any manner whatsoever without written permission except in the case of reprints in the context of reviews. For information, write Andrews McMeel Publishing, an Andrews McMeel Universal company, 4520 Main Street, Kansas City, Missouri 64111.

ISBN 0-7407-5544-7

courtesy of Tali and Ophira Edut, www.theastrotwins.com

"Carmella's Ziti," pp. 24–25, from The Sopranos Family Cookbook by Artie Bucco and Allen Rucker. Copyright © 2002 by Warner Books, Inc. By permission of Warner Books, Inc.

Attention: Schools and Businesses

Andrews McMeel books are available at quantity discounts with
bulk purchase for educational, business, or sales promotional use.
For information, please write to: Special Sales Department,
Andrews McMeel Publishing, 4520 Main Street, Kansas City, Missouri 64111.

For Keith

Acknowledgments

I was not so much the author for this book as the self-appointed magnet for great ideas. An enormous roster of friends proffered their favorite flavors of romance. The best ones made it through this gauntlet of Cabernet-sipping fun police: Rebecca Asher Walsh, Karen Hamilton, Hilary Black, Meredith Berkman, Virginia de Liagre, Barbara Graham, Susan O'Keefe, Sheila Buckmaster, Margaret Bergen, Annie Griffiths Belt, and Allison Smiley. Thanks so much to my agent, Claudia Cross; my editor, Kelly Gilbert; and artists Mary Claire Smith and Nina Edwards, who brought these ideas to life. Thanks to Vivian Deushel and all of our friends at the Ritz-Carlton. Thanks also to my trusty researcher, Keren Sachs. And my most heartfelt gratitude goes to my husband, Keith Bellows, my ultimate partner-in-crime for all things divine.

Introduction

In my single days, during the excruciatingly long, thirstier-than-the-Sahara dry spells between suitors, I discovered something that saved me: I was never actually lonely—as long as I was having fun. In *The Fun Book: 102 Ways for Girls to Have Some*, I proposed an obvious if empowering truth: Fun is a single girl's best friend. Possible anytime, anywhere, even when you least expect it, fun is a Zen master when it comes to reducing stress, a zippy shortcut to living in the moment, and a stealth bomber to life's cruelest indignities. The most chivalrous Prince Charming, fun never lets you down—even when life does.

Just when I was getting the hang of things—riding around in ragtops with girlfriends, perfecting the dirty martini, and amusing myself by using my ex-boyfriend's very favorite T-shirt to clean the bathroom floor—everything changed. It happened on a rainy night plucked from the files of when-you-least-expect-it. (And believe me, I was not ready for my close-up.)

The following day I was scheduled to leave for France, where I had a writing assignment to cover the Cannes Film Festival for the *New York Times* Style section. I was unpacked, overweight, and more than mildly stressed.

Maintaining my commitment to fun, however, I had R.S.V.P.'d to attend a book signing that night. I was grateful that the affair was for a chick book, rendering the presence of testosterone unlikely, and I wouldn't know a soul in the sophisticated, who's-your-agent? crowd anyway. My plan was to lurk in the back and slip out as soon as my book was signed.

That's when the door banged open and— cue the music, please—in walked the most beautiful man I had ever seen in my life!

Tall and tan, with laserlike green eyes and longish salt-and-pepper hair, he strode toward the author with the alpha dog confidence of a movie star. I quickly hid behind a magazine.

The hostess handed me a glass of wine, leaned in, and murmured, "The real reason I wanted you here is to meet Keith Bellows. He's *almost* single." Now considering the only two men in room were her husband and the Tall Tan Stranger, I knew exactly whom she was talking about.

Gulp.

I hightailed it to the door. My hand was on the knob when I felt a grip on my shoulder. As I turned around, I heard the words I was dreading.

"Melina, I'd like to introduce you to Keith. Both of you are with magazines and I'm sure you have a lot in common," said Barbara before disappearing.

My mind zoomed to what we did not have in common. Namely, a tiara of frizz, sticking straight up from my forehead. On the way to the book signing, I had wedged in a visit to my hairdresser, who had only had time to chop my bangs without bothering to wet them down first. The effect was Rosanne Rosanadana at best. The other thing that we didn't have in common was a strange white shape above my upper lip. That's because my mustache wax effectively eliminated the Frida Kahlo look—along with the pre-Cannes self-tanner I had been applying all week.

Triage: Immediately, I blocked my bangs with my left hand, and strategically hid my mouth behind my wineglass. I managed a muffled "Nize-to-meetu" from behind my Chardonnay, calmly reassuring myself we'd be out of small talk in a nanosecond.

The next thing you know, the hostess was asking us to leave. Somehow, three hours had passed, but Keith and I were so submerged in Deep Flirt that we hadn't even noticed that the entire party had evaporated. This man was so charming that I didn't care about any of the red flags he had mentioned, including that his divorce was not final, he spent every weekend with his son in Tennessee, and—the clincher—he lived several states away, rendering him Geographically Undesirable.

So what if he wasn't The One. I had the time of my life! If nothing else, it was a fabulous case of Talk at First Sight. Keith was a sign to have hope: Great men are not, as I was beginning to suspect, a myth like Bigfoot and the Loch Ness monster. I just had to find one like him who happened to live in New York.

The next day when I walked into my office, I was

greeted by an enormous bouquet of sunflowers and an e-mail invitation to continue our conversation over dinner. We embarked on a courtship that lifted fun to an art form. I wrote in *The Fun Book* that fun grows exponentially when shared. It's true: All of the fun I was having while I was single more than doubled with Keith. After all, what could possibly be more fun than falling in love?

Any time we had together we treated as precious. We relished introducing each other to our favorite people, restaurants, cocktails, and places. We kissed our way through movies, and we rode through revolving doors together, always. Our favorite game was delighting each other. I planned a fall weekend at a b&b on Shelter Island, a gem in the Long Island Sound, where we slurped oysters, went antiquing, and strolled for hours on the deserted beach. A month later, he returned the favor by inviting me for a drink at a hot new boutique hotel. He had booked a suite and filled it with tiny votive candles and hidden beautifully wrapped Christmas presents hidden all over the room. The last two I unwrapped were a bottle of Veuve Clicquot and red silk pajamas.

Within a year we became engaged, and eight months later we were married. Over the course of our courtship, however, I realized something ironic. The tail was wagging the dog. True, fun grows when shared, but it's the *partnership* that grows when two people have fun together.

First of all, fun is the best way to bond. Starting a life together in Washington, D.C., provided the perfect excuse to figure out new ways to amuse ourselves. Because we didn't know anyone, we threw ourselves into couple dating. We had a "say yes" attitude that the *Rules* girls would have forbidden. But we got to hang out with an eclectic cross-section of people who enlightened us on everything from the best farmer's markets to the tastiest ethnic restaurants inside the Beltway.

Fun also provided a way for Keith and me to get to know each other better. By trial and error, we discovered that while we are compatible in our appetites, we don't always choose the same flavor. For example, while Keith loves surprises, I prefer looking forward to something. True, I almost had a nervous breakdown surprising him with a sailboat for his birthday. But when we pulled up behind the blue and white, twenty-foot O'Day that had his pet name painted on the stern, the look on his face was worth the stress of keeping such a big secret.

Knowing from past debacles that I hate surprises, Keith sweetly kept me in the loop about the Tuscan feast he was planning for my birthday. But he parted with each detail as if he was passing a gall stone.

"Uhhhh, Rudy and Olivia are coming." Wince, wince, grimace, grimace.

Deep breath. "And I was thinking we'd serve the special Burgundies we've been saving." Long sigh.

But in a way, it's sort of a *Gift of the Magi* in martyrdom. While we truly appreciate the lengths we go to in order to please each other, the giggle fits that come with knowing each other's idiosyncrasies are almost as good as the gifts themselves.

In fact, the more intimate we've become as a couple, the more we've realized that fun does not need to be extravagant. Some of our favorite ways to have fun have actually been free.

Even the smallest gestures can act as an invaluable insurance policy for a relationship. I know from watching my parents, who have been married for forty years, that a couple that *plays* together *stays* together. Sure, they do weird things, like turn up the ABBA so loud that the car actually vibrates as they do their errands. And particular specimens of my father's hat collection, which can make appearances at any time (like Keith's first visit), never fail to make my otherwise model-of-decorum mother into a giggling, whooping lunatic. But belly laughs, they both swear, have been the magic to their marriage.

As I discovered the night I met Keith, something as simple as a serious flirt can hit the spot. But there are countless ways to court a good time. In fact, the simple quiet pleasure of just being together can be an invitation to joy. After all, what better way than fun to celebrate love every day? As Mark Twain said, "To get the full value of joy, you must have someone to divide it with."

Make *angels* in the snow.
   Before getting back into the hot tub.

Perfect the art of snuggling.

You will need:

1. a cashmere blanket
2. very old sweats, preferably from college
3. a scented candle (if possible, splurge on a Diptyque)
4. one very large, deep couch
5. Van Morrison, Ella Fitzgerald, Miles Davis, Billie Holiday CDs

Keep a boom box in the kitchen.

Slow dance while you are making dinner. (Or coffee.)

Go shopping for new sunglasses together.

Imagine you are movie stars (or spies) as you wear them.

"Imagination is the highest kite one can fly."
—LAUREN BACALL

While shopping together at a large grocery or hardware store, pretend you have to use the ladies' room and break away. Have him paged from the info desk.

Use his most embarrassing pet name.

Check into a fabulous hotel.

Register under a  *phony name,* arrive separately,
and pretend you're movie stars having an affair.

Grant each other one "Get Out of Jail Free" card.
When he does something really stupid,
let him cash it in. You get the same privilege.

"Love is the triumph of imagination over intelligence."

—H. L. MENCKEN

Create a Sunday morning ritual. Have the *New York Times* delivered, play Bach's Bandeberg concerti, and make Belgian waffles and fresh-squeezed grapefruit juice. Promise yourselves you won't do anything productive until after three P.M.

"Any time that is not spent on love is wasted."

—TORQUATO TASSO

For his next birthday, have a pal take an artsy black-and-white photo of you. **In the nude.**

Discover your inner Julia Child with a series of in-home cooking lessons *à deux*. Check newspapers, go online, or call the chef of your favorite restaurant to make a house call. Then wow your pals with a multicourse gourmet meal.

"Life itself is the proper binge."

—JULIA CHILD

Take to the waters together. Add *lavender bath oil, rose petals, bubbles,* and *bubbly* as needed. Wash each other's hair. Watch Meryl Streep and Robert Redford in *Out of Africa* for inspiration.

Send him a bouquet of flowers at the office "just because." Do it on a Monday so they last all week, and make sure the arrangement is large enough that his coworkers can smell it down the hall.

How to say it with flowers:

BELLS OF IRELAND * good luck
CAMELLIA * perfection
COTTAGE PINK * divine love
FORGET-ME-NOT * remembrance
IVY * eternal fidelity
LILY-OF-THE-VALLEY * return of happiness
PINK CARNATION * I'll never forget you
PRIMROSE * I can't live without you
RED CARNATION * admiration
RED POPPY * pleasure
RED ROSE * passion
RED TULIP * declaration of love
STEPHANOTIS * happiness in marriage
YARROW * my headache is gone

Start a monthly girls' night out. Encourage him to have a boys' night out. Come home and be all the more grateful that you are together.

"The way to love anything is to realize that it might be lost."

—G. K. CHESTERTON

Plan a room-service weekend in your home.

Declare a proverbial "Do not disturb." Turn off the ringer on the phone, and ignore your mail and e-mail. Lounge around in brand-new, thick, white cotton terry robes. Watch the Travel Channel and pretend you are in the exotic destination of your choice. Stock the "maxibar" with all the usual suspects, everything from beverages galore to gourmet chocolate to a disposable camera, and order in all of your meals. Don't forget to make a pit stop at your video store so that you can command movies on demand without having to leave home.

Make friends with the manager of your local wine shop. Have a monthly date with your "personal sommelier" to introduce you to the latest bargains from around the world. Then buy a lottery ticket. When you get home, add cheese as necessary. As you sip and munch, muse about all of the things you will do with the winnings.

DYNAMIC DUOS:

Brie ✱ cabernet sauvignon
Camembert ✱ pinot noir
Cheddar ✱ Syrah
Chèvre ✱ sauvignon blanc
Feta ✱ chardonnay
Gorgonzola ✱ Syrah, Rhône, zinfandel
Gruyère ✱ pinot noir
Parmesan ✱ Chianti
Pecorino ✱ zinfandel

"Wine comes in at the mouth; love comes in through the eye."

—HENRI MATISSE

Give him a gift certificate to your favorite lingerie store.

Make a date to let him unwrap your presence.

"Love is the same as like except you feel sexier."

—JUDITH VIORST

Take a "personal day" together. Spend an entire morning in bed writing your dream list of couple goals, like adventuring on an African safari, buying a sailboat, riding in a hot-air balloon, or owning a b&b. Agree on a few priorities and put the list on the fridge. Make love to seal the deal.

"When two people love each other, they don't look at each other, they look in the same direction."

—GINGER ROGERS

Before a summer party, ask him to paint each of your toenails a different color. Show off your custom Picasso toes.

Buy him a pair of tickets to his favorite sporting event.

AT-HOME VERSION: Seat him in front of the TV with his favorite beer and a big bowl of popcorn. Announce that halftime is yours, with instructions to meet you in the bedroom. Wear nothing but a jersey from his favorite team and tell him it's his turn to score. Coach as necessary.

Dazzle him with one piece of obscure trivia.

Read his horoscope to him every day. E-mail it to him when he's out of town. (P.S. Screen the bad ones.) If he seems to like this, get your charts done by an astrologer.

Star-powered Astro-Matches

Your Sign	*Whom You Love*	*Stuff You're Made Of*
Aries	Sagittarius and Leo	fire
Taurus	Virgo and Capricorn	earth
Gemini	Libra and Aquarius	air
Cancer	Scorpio and Pisces	water
Leo	Aries and Sagittarius	fire
Virgo	Taurus and Capricorn	earth
Libra	Aquarius and Gemini	air
Scorpio	Cancer and Pisces	water
Sagittarius	Aries and Leo	fire
Capricorn	Taurus and Virgo	earth
Aquarius	Gemini and Libra	air
Pisces	Cancer and Scorpio	water

Signs of the same "element" (fire, water, etc.) often get along the best, usually because there's more of you to love! Of course, opposites attract—a person of a different element may have some important lessons to teach you, so always follow your heart.

Rent a sailboat for a day.
Pack a picnic and don't forget the champagne.

In England there's a tradition called the Tuesday gift, which is a little gift for no reason. Be like the Brits and get him something small but thoughtful. Send it to his office, or leave it on the seat of his car.

"There is but one genuine love potion—consideration."

—MENANDER

On a rainy Saturday, rent *The Sopranos* on DVD. Make Carmella's Ziti so you can escape to the kitchen during the violent parts. Here's how.

Serves 8–12

* 1 pound ziti
* salt
* about 5 cups of your favorite red sauce
* 1 cup freshly grated pecorino, Romano, or Parmigiano-Reggiano cheese
* 1 cup ricotta cheese
* 8 ounces mozzarella cheese, cut into small dice

Preheat the oven to 350°F.

Bring at least 4 quarts of water to a boil in a large pot. Add the ziti and salt to taste. Cook, stirring frequently, until the ziti is *al dente*—tender yet firm to the bite. Drain the ziti and put it in a large bowl. Toss it with about 3 cups of the red sauce and $1/2$ cup of the grated cheese.

Spoon half the ziti into a shallow $3\,1/2$-quart baking dish. Spread the ricotta on top and sprinkle with the mozzarella and $1/4$ cup of the grated cheese. Pour on 1 cup of the sauce. Top with the remaining ziti and another cup of sauce. Sprinkle with the remaining grated cheese. Cover the dish with foil. (The ziti can be refrigerated for several hours, or overnight, at this point. Remove from the refrigerator about 30 minutes before baking.)

Bake the ziti for 45 minutes. Uncover and bake for 15 to 30 minutes longer, or until the center is hot and the sauce is bubbling around the edges. Cover and let stand for 15 minutes before serving.

Take a time-out to change perspectives. Have a weekly standing date to walk and talk. After dinner, just take off. If possible, make the kids do the dishes while you share the details of your day, the week's challenges, and upcoming plans to have fun.

"Love doesn't sit there, like a stone; it has to be made, like bread, remade all the time, made new."

—URSULA K. LE GUIN

Enjoy the symphony
of comfortable silence.

Scour the newspapers for cheap flights to Paris. Rent the film *Amélie* first to get excited.

Once you get there, here's the to-do list:

1. Beg, borrow, or steal enough money to spend at least a night at Hôtel de Crillon.
2. Buy a toy sailboat to launch in the Jardin du Luxembourg.

3. Window-shop on the avenue Montaigne

4. Do Jelly shots at the bar at the Plaza Athénée. (Locals call it the Blue Bar.)

5.  Go to the Musée d'Orsay and pick your favorite Renoir.

6. Sip hot chocolate at Les Deux Magots and pretend you are Jean-Paul Sartre and Simone de Beauvoir.

7. Stroll through the sculpture garden at the Musée Rodin. Emulate **The Kiss**.

8. Lingerie-shop at Sabbia Rosa.

9. Eat crepes from a street vendor as you stroll the weekend flea market.

10. Visit the Mona Lisa at the Louvre. Gaze at her smile, and whisper naughty things to each other. Imagine that she is eavesdropping.

Kidnap him for a long weekend.

(If possible, call his office and tell them he won't be in on Monday, either.)

Pack his bag, book a room at an inn, and call ahead to arrange to have his favorite drink chilling in the room. Pop in your personal soundtrack and hit the road. Don't tell him anything. Everything is as authentic as a kidnapping, except he isn't kicking to get out of your car trunk.

Listen to the
Harry Potter book series
on audiocassette together.

(It's like being read to as a child.)

Make a pact to believe in magic again.

Host a "diner" party in your kitchen. Invite guests to come in their comfiest clothes. Write the menu on a blackboard, and find a country-Western station on the radio. Make my mom's meat loaf, and serve it with mashed potatoes and banana cream pie. Don't forget to use paper napkins and plastic cups. Move out the living room furniture so you can dance afterward.

SUZI GEROSA'S MOJO MEAT LOAF

Mix together:

* 2 pounds ground meat—1/3 beef, 1/3 pork, 1/3 veal
* 5 pieces stale Italian bread
* 3 eggs
* 1 onion, chopped and sautéed
* 1/3 cup milk
* 2 teaspoons salt
* 2 teaspoons pepper
* 1 teaspoon garlic powder
* 1/3 cup ketchup

Preheat the oven to 350 degrees. Mix all the ingredients except ketchup thoroughly. Shape the mixture into a loaf. Make a slight indentation in the top down the length of the loaf. Pour ketchup into the indentation. Bake for 1 hour and 30 minutes in a 9 x 12 roasting pan.

Play *Pretty Woman.*

Go to very fancy shops, where you would never actually buy anything, and *invite him to come into the dressing room* with you while you model the latest couture. Let the saleswoman think he's your sugar daddy.

Go night skiing or ice-skating.
Warm each other up when you get home.

Keep a book of poems on the nightstand.

Take turns reading to each other before going to sleep.

POETS WHO KNOW IT

❋ Rainer Maria Rilke ❋
❋ Pablo Neruda ❋
❋ William Shakespeare ❋
❋ Robert Frost ❋
❋ Emily Dickinson ❋
❋ W. B. Yeats ❋
❋ Anne Bradstreet ❋
❋ John Keats ❋
❋ Walt Whitman ❋

"I want to do with you what spring does with the cherry trees."

—PABLO NERUDA

Arrange a playdate with your inner children. Hit the swings at the playground, fingerpaint, jump on a trampoline. Play nice. Or naughty.

"Make sure your heart is awake when you are having fun."

—DYLAN O'KEEFE, AGE FIVE

Twenty-one days before Christmas, give him an advent calendar. Personalize it by putting compliments, ego boosts, photographs, and lascivious comments where the little pictures of angels and the little drummer boy should be.

"To love is to place our happiness in the happiness of another."

—GOTTFRIED WILHELM LEIBNIZ

Be coconspirators and host a James Bond martini party. Play James Bond videos (sans sound) on your TV. Imagine you are Pussy Galore, Jinx, or the Bond girl of your choice as you and your spy guy shake up these tasty martinis for your friends.

007 JAMES BOND VODKA MARTINI

- 2 ounces vodka
- ¾ ounce dry vermouth

Shake the vodka and vermouth over ice and strain into martini glasses. Garnish with an olive and serve. Remember, "Shaken, not stirred." Makes 1 serving.

THE VESPER

(as ordered by Bond in *Casino Royale*)

- 3 parts Gordon's gin
- 1 part vodka
- ½ part Kina Lillet vermouth

Shake all ingredients over ice. Pour into deep champagne goblets. Garnish with a thin slice of lemon peel. Makes 1 serving.

CUCUMBER COSMOPOLITAN

(from Restaurant August, New Orleans)

- ❋ ¾-inch slice cucumber, puréed
- ❋ 2 ounces Ketel One vodka
- ❋ ¾ ounce Cointreau
- ❋ ½ ounce lime juice
- ❋ Splash of cranberry juice

Shake all the ingredients over ice. Strain into a martini glass, and garnish with a slice of cucumber. Makes 1 serving.

VEGAS LEMON DROP

* 2 ounces Absolut Citron
* 1 ounce triple Sec
* 1 ounce lime juice

Use a lemon slice to wet the rim of a well-chilled martini glass. Dip the glass in white sugar until coated. Shake the ingredients over ice and strain into the prepared glass. Makes 1 serving.

LAVA LAMP MARTINI

* 2 ounces vodka
* ½ ounce raspberry liqueur
* 1 tablespoon honey

Mix the liqueur with the honey in a shot glass. Pour the vodka into a shaker with ice and shake. Strain into a martini glass and spoon in the honey mixture. Makes 1 serving.

When booking travel accommodations, say it's your honeymoon.

(You might get room or flight upgrades, or free champagne.)

Always act like it is.

P.S. Keep track of where and when you do this so you won't get busted.

Do something nice for someone in his family. Help his sister with her résumé, or take his mom out for tea. Don't tell him.

"I expect to pass through life but once. If therefore, there be any kindness I can show . . . let me do it now."

—WILLIAM PENN

Take turns playing slave, domestic or sexual, for a night.

"It's not the men in my life, it's the life in my men."

—MAE WEST

Go for a fall drive and play your old cassettes from high school. Pull over at the scenic overlook and "park" for a while.

Stargaze during a meteor shower. Bring warm blankets and hot chocolate with Kahlúa. Make wishes together and for each other.

"To love is to receive a glimpse of heaven."

—KAREN SUNDE

Have an aphrodisiac night.
Ply him with oysters and champagne.

Add other aphrodisiacs as needed.

garlic ✸ truffles

asparagus ✸ caviar

pomegranates ✸ chocolate

honey ✸ figs

pine nuts ✸ ginger

grapes ✸ strawberries

tomatoes ✸ bull testicles

green M&M's

P.S. If you can't find bull testicles, listening to him as if he's the only man on earth has equally potent effects.

Celebrate summer— make love al fresco.

"The Loving are the Daring."

—BAYARD TAYLOR

Leave him *"pocket notes"* in surprising places, like under his pillow or in his wallet. Be specific with your *"I love you."* Write something you really appreciate about him, thank him for something he did for you recently, or cut out a *New Yorker* cartoon that you know he'd really get.

𝓜eet him at home for a
"hot lunch."

"Love is merely a madness . . ."
—WILLIAM SHAKESPEARE

Celebrate the anniversary of the day that you first met.

Bake him his favorite cookies.

Help each other get dressed for a **black-tie** event.

Learn to do his bow tie, and let him figure out how to clasp your pearls. Surprise him with a white rose boutonniere.

Buy him beautifully engraved stationery.

Write the first note and leave it in the box for him to discover.

Develop a secret language. Learn to speak in code when other people are around. Goal: From across the room, he should be able to catch your stinkbomb eyeball about that egregious fashion faux pas you've spotted.

"Shared laughter is erotic too."

—MARGE PIERCY

Make Sunday night dinner special.

Light a candle, play music, and use a linen napkin, even if you are eating a salad. Take time to enjoy each other before charging into another hectic week.

Go shoe shopping together.

Let him pick out a pair of *sexy* high heels.
Then let your walking do the talking.

Find a great barber and give him the gift of an old-fashioned shave.

Host a paella party.

Invite your guests into the kitchen to cook with you. Play Latin groove and serve sangria as everyone chops and dices. Call him the sexy Spanish name of your choice for the evening.

Encourage spontaneous flamenco dancing.

Volunteer together. Find one cause you are both passionate about. Be a screener for the golden retriever dog rescue, rent clown costumes and visit the pediatric ward, or work in a soup kitchen on Christmas Eve.

"What do we live for, if it is not to make life less difficult for each other?"

—GEORGE ELIOT

Go for his-and-hers pedicures together.

Bring a bottle of Chardonnay and paper cups.
(If he objects, tell him it's a "sports pedicure.")

Get certified to scuba dive and play with the fishes. It's one of the few sports where men don't have a physical advantage over women, plus you can spend lots of time together and you don't even have to talk (which is handy if you are having a fight).

GREAT DIVING SPOTS AROUND THE WORLD

Ambergris Caye ✱ Belize
Bonaire ✱ Netherlands Antilles
Cozumel ✱ Mexico
Grand Cayman ✱ British West Indies
Phuket ✱ Thailand
Rangiroa ✱ Tahiti
Rowley Shoals ✱ Australia's northwest coast
Truk Lagoon ✱ Micronesia

Next Thanksgiving, give him a thank-you basket. Pack a basket with all things to let him know how much you truly appreciate him—massage oil, the latest thriller by his favorite author, and a fun pair of boxers. Everything should be inexpensive, but extra thoughtful.

"Love is, above all, the gift of oneself."

—JEAN ANOUILH

Give up one habit that drives each other bonkers.

He goes first.

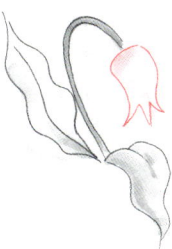

"Great love too must be endured."

—COCO CHANEL

Practice the art of aromatherapy together.

Drop by Jo Malone, L'Occitane, or a specialty boutique and try on scents for each other. Splurge on lotions, shampoos, and fragrances. Don't forget about your home: Incense, scented candles, and oils add instant atmosphere.

SCENTS AND SENSIBILITY

CARDAMOM ✻ *warms and invigorates*
GINGER ✻ *stimulant, increases sexual interest, relieves headaches*
JASMINE ✻ *instills a sense of romance*
LAVENDER ✻ *calms and relaxes*
LEMON ✻ *improves alertness*
PEPPERMINT ✻ *uplifts and refreshes*
ROSEMARY ✻ *soothes the nervous system*
SANDALWOOD ✻ *restores balance*
YLANG YLANG ✻ *increases sexual interest and energy*

Play gardener for a day.

You both point, he digs. Enjoy growing things together.
No backyard? Tend herbs on a windowsill.

Keep a disposable camera on hand for those indisposable moments. Photo tips from *National Geographic*'s Photographer-in-Residence Annie Griffiths Belt.

1. Get closer. What you will want to see in years to come are those beautiful faces, not their shoes!

2. When photographing groups, get people to touch one another. It gives them something to do with their hands.

3. Avoid photographing people in bright sunshine. Harsh light is not flattering, and nobody looks good squinting!

4. There is nothing more wonderful than seeing the person you love asleep. Take photos of unguarded and happy moments too.

"Christen"

a new car or home.

Master the art of the striptease.

1. Make a date with him, and set the mood with candles, music, and champagne.
2. Wear a beautiful lingerie set under a silk teddy and high heels. Use a prop, like a feather boa or his favorite necktie.
3. Have him sit on the bed, and keep distance between the two of you to build tension.
4. Imagine you are Catherine Zeta-Jones as you begin to dance around.
5. Smile, never break eye contact, and shimmy.
6. To the beat of the music, slowly take off the teddy and toss it at him.
7. Smile. Repeat and remove all of your clothing.

"All serious daring starts from within."

—EUDORA WELTY

Start a collection together.

Scour flea markets, yard sales, and travel destinations to expand your collection. Some fun things to collect: etched wine glasses, local artwork, sterling silver picture frames, antique leather-bound books.

> **P.S.** We like to collect the secrets of success of the happily married couples we admire.

Start a book club for two.

Required reading:

The Kama Sutra.

Have a guy/girl film festival.

Here are twenty movies that will satisfy both.

Adaptation ✸ *Airplane!*
The American President ✸ *Analyze This*
As Good as It Gets ✸ *Austin Powers, The Spy Who Shagged Me*
Being John Malkovich ✸ *Best in Show*
Big Night ✸ *Chicago*
Frida ✸ *Godfather* series
L.A. Confidential ✸ *Lord of the Rings* series
Moulin Rouge ✸ *Naked Gun* series
The Patriot ✸ *The Sixth Sense*
Waiting for Guffman ✸ *When Harry Met Sally*

These will backfire: Don't attempt!

How to Lose a Guy in Ten Days ✷ *Love Story*
Sleepless in Seattle ✷ *The Way We Were*
While You Were Sleeping

And don't let him talk you into these:

Bad Lieutenant ✷ *Monty Python* series
Reservoir Dogs ✷ *Natural Born Killers*
Scarface

Pull him into a photo booth and *kiss* for the *camera*.

Tuck the little black and whites in his car visor or somewhere you know he'll see it often.

Be culture vultures, high and low. Get decked out and go to the opera, theater, symphony, or ballet together. Celebrate your cultural evolution afterward by dining at your favorite burger joint.

Play truth or dare.

Or just dare.

"If you obey all the rules you miss all the fun."

— KATHARINE HEPBURN

Overdo it on his favorite treat. Does he love Girl Scout cookies? Order him a case. Golf addict? Buy him boxes and boxes of his favorite balls.

"Too much of a good thing is wonderful."

—MAE WEST

Go to an open house or get an agent to take you to check out real estate together.

Pretend you're rich and enjoy checking out other people's homes.

Rub each other the right way.

Plan a massage night. Take turns inventing new techniques on each other. Better yet, splurge on a spa.

Save an "emergency" week of vacation time for when the airlines have cheap flights to Rome. Then make your way to Venice. Watch *Roman Holiday* before you go.

TO DO LIST

1. Sit on the terrace of the Gritti palace. Drink Bellinis (champagne and peach nectar) as you watch the canal.

2. Hold hands and skip through the pigeons in the Piazza San Marco at night.

3. Eat cuttlefish risotto at Da Ivo.

4. Marvel at the marble at San Cico church.

5. Stroll through the Peggy Guggenheim museum and pick your favorite sculpture.

6. Serenade back a gondola driver.

7. Have the launch take you to dinner at Harry Cipriani, where Hemingway hung out.

8. Buy two handmade masks. Weave them into your late-night activities.

9. Instead of a sit-down dinner, stroll around the city, stopping a couple of times for slices of pizza, gelato, and cappuccino.

Pretend you've never met each other.
Go to a bar and play out the scene.

Surprise him by showing up in a wig.

Hike under a full moon.

SOME COOL NATIONAL PARKS TO EXPLORE:

1. Acadia National Park, Maine
2. Glacier National Park, Montana
3. Grand Canyon National Park, Arizona
4. Grand Teton National Park, Wyoming
5. Great Smoky Mountains National Park, North Carolina and Tennessee
6. Olympic National Park, Washington
7. Rocky Mountain National Park, Colorado
8. Yellowstone National Park, Wyoming
9. Yosemite National Park, California
10. Zion National Park, Utah

People-watch.

Invent elaborate identities for the people you observe. Take turns describing the who, what, when, and where, and then add the reason they were recently featured in the *National Enquirer* or the police blotter.

Hula dance for him.

In Hawaii, it's a wedding tradition for a bride to learn a special hula dance for her husband. A tip for beginners: Try this right out of the shower wearing nothing but a towel around your waist.

Get box seats for a sporting event,
making sure you two have the box to
yourselves so that you can canoodle
to the cheers of the crowd.

Tell him that you had the most *incredible, sexy dream* about him the night before.

(This does not have to be true to be effective.)

Describe it in great detail.

Indulge his dreams.

Send him to the school of his choice.

SOME FUN ONES:

EXTREME SKIING/SNOWBOARDING SCHOOL

MOUNTAIN-CLIMBING SCHOOL ✽ RACE-CAR DRIVER SCHOOL

RODEO SCHOOL ✽ SCUBA-DIVING SCHOOL

SKY-DIVING SCHOOL ✽ SURFER SCHOOL

"We love because it's the only true adventure."

—NIKKI GIOVANNI

Go shopping together for your new perfume.
You squirt, he sniffs.

"Taking joy in life is a woman's best cosmetic."

—ROSALIND RUSSELL

Pick your favorite food to eat out, like ribs or Indian food. Then become aficionados, and try every different restaurant in your area.

Take yoga together.
Do it downward-doggy style.

Etch your initials in a heart under the kitchen table

(or under the dining room table if you are really committed).

"The mark of a true crush . . . is that you fall in love first and grope for reasons afterward."

—SHANA ALEXANDER

Rent a bicycle built for two. Pack an exquisite picnic for the basket and don't forget a blanket.

$\mathcal{W}$hen you are in love, nothing heightens the experience like the energy of New York City. Here's a lovers to-do list:

1. Catch a movie at the Ziegfeld Theater. Pick a late afternoon matinee so when you leave the theater it's dark outside.

2. Visit the Metropolitan Museum of Art. Check out the Temple of Dendur and the French Impressionism wing before heading up to the rooftop bar to scope the sculptures (and the singles scene).

3. Get steaming hot bagels and stroll the promenade of the East River while the sun is rising.

4. Go to Times Square and stand in line for half-price tickets to a Broadway show. That night, get decked out and spend the money you saved on cocktails and appetizers at Palio. (The outrageous, bright red, wraparound mural of charging horses comes for free.)

5. On a Saturday afternoon, head to Zabar's on the Upper West Side. Put together a picnic and then plop near the boathouse in Central Park. Enjoy your wine and cheese all the more watching the überexercisers whirl by on bikes and in-line skates and with baby joggers.

6. Stroll around Soho on a Sunday afternoon. Wander in and out of shops and galleries and enjoy an early dinner at an outside café.

7. Take a sidetrip to City Island. Eat lobsters and drink beer while you watch the boats go by.

8. Take a pedicab. The wind whips through your hair as your bike-riding driver whisks you around the city streets.

9. Go to a funky bar (like the Other Room in the West Village) with no plans and a *Time Out* magazine and decide what you'll do that evening.

10. Or check into the Ritz-Carlton New York, Central Park. And never leave the room.

Always jump into his slot
when he goes through a revolving door.
Remember, what goes around comes around.

Watch the Academy Awards together.

Drink champagne and eat little pizzas like they do at Morton's, where legendary Hollywood agent Swifty Lazar used to host an annual bash. Don't forget to give him a special award of his own.

Get in the habit of thanking him for every single thing he does for you, large or small.

Transform your bedroom into a soothing sanctuary.
Paint it a tranquil color, like celadon green or cerulean blue. Make sure the lighting is exactly the way you want it, with the appropriate blinds, curtains, and, of course, candles. Outfit your bed with a wardrobe of Egyptian cotton, 400-plus–thread count sheets. Find the perfect pillows. Tuck lavender-scented sachets inside the pillowcases. Keep bottled water and a bowl of clementines handy for a pre-bedtime snack. Keep the radio on a classical or jazz station.

Fun and funny are two different things.

Ask him what's fun and/or what's funny about various people, places, situations, and pets. Fun or funny? You two decide.

Get the pet appropriate to your commitment level.

Start with a goldfish and work your way up.

The puppy needs to come with a prenup.

Take him to test-drive
the car of his dreams.

Nap in
each other's arms.
In a hammock.

Buy every CD that he doesn't have of his favorite artist.

Take dance lessons together. Don't tell friends, and surprise them with your Fred-and-Ginger moves the next time you hit the dance floor.

"Nothing is more revealing than movement."

—MARTHA GRAHAM

Spend a rainy afternoon wandering around a bookstore together. Buy each other a book before leaving.

Surprise him by meeting him at the airport.

Wear a trench coat and sunglasses and hold up a sign with his name on it.

Figure out what really scares him. Don't let him know that you know, but be on the lookout so you can be his loyal guardian angel, on the ready to bring him comfort.

"True strength is delicate."

—LOUISE NEVELSON

Take a late-night walk on the local golf course.

(It's spooky and exciting.)

Make sure one of you has a good sense of direction.

On his next birthday,
go to the library and copy the headlines
from the day he was born.

Pillow talk. Snuggle up and check in with each other. Ask him if he's getting enough sex, time with you, and even alone time. Tell him what you need too.

$\mathcal{E}$very anniversary, renew your fun vows. Commit to one fun thing the two of you will do that week, that month, and that year.

"There is only one happiness in life, to love and be loved."

—GEORGE SAND